PREPARING FOR MARRIAGE

The Secrets to Long Lasting Relationship and Marriage

EZEKIEL UGBEDA

Preparing for Marriage: The Secrets to Long Lasting Relationships and Marriage by Ezekiel Ugbeda

Published by Ezekiel Ugbeda

CONTACT
Ugbedaezekiel200@gmail.com
+2349036845604 & +2349029863386

ISBN: 978-978-791-670-4

Printed in the Federal Republic of Nigeria

DEDICATION

To everyone who is aspiring to have a glorious and successful marriage.

ACKNOWLEDGEMENT

I sincerely want to appreciate everyone for your relentless efforts and contributions toward the publication of this book.

First and foremost, I would like to appreciate God Almighty, who has given me the knowledge, wisdom, and revelation to write this book through his infinite Mercy.

Secondly, I want to sincerely thank my Dad, Mr Williams Ugbeda and my mum, Mrs Grace Ugbeda, who through divine wisdom, have set a solid foundation for their 8 Children. This great wisdom has made me become a responsible man today.

I will like to appreciate my wonderful siblings (Peace, Favour, Miracle, Moses, Faith, Samuel and Happiness) for your constant support, encouragement and love.

I appreciate the Members, Elders and the Pastoral Team of United Evangelical Church (UEC) Dei- Dei branch, specifically my Spiritual Leaders, Elder Jonah Musa and Pastor Stephen Edibo, for your Spiritual Coverage.

My wonderful friend, Bro Enemona Onyeke, thank you for your unquantifiable contribution to my life. You are not just a mere friend, but a brother indeed and a destiny helper.

I also appreciate my dignified mentors, Mrs Bassey Victory, Mrs Naomi Chinyere Ihejirika, Miss Mercy Emmanuel, Miss Grace Emmanuel, Miss Nora Amara Ekperinwa, Bro Simon Ojimah and Apostle Ezekiel Agbali, for your mentoring, training and discipling.

I wish to appreciate my Exceptional friends, Emmanuel Joshua, Elizabeth Jonah, Benjamin Kashio, Susan Joshua, Augustine Itegi, Ibrahim Yayajo, Grace Ezekiel, Benjamin Ejeh Sunday, Simon chuks, Rebecca Abraham, Lawrence James, Simon Joel, Emmanuel Eniwaye, Ali King Arome, Ogundele Joshua, for your motivation and encouragement.

I want to appreciate everyone out there whose name is not mentioned.

INTRODUCTION.

Are you aware that many young people have given up on love relationships due to several heartbreaks? Are you also aware that many successful people in Business, Politics, Careers, and even in Ministry have been unable to find the right life partner? Do you know that several married couples worldwide today live in pain and regrets simply because they married wrongly? Many of them wished they had the requisite knowledge before going into the relationship and marriage they are in now but didn't get the opportunity to right those wrongs.

This book will correct those wrong decisions you have made in the past. It will help you understand the secrets to long-lasting relationships and marriage and help you understand the purpose of marriage and ways to sustain your relationship and marriage. The book will give you the maximum wisdom and understanding to guide you in choosing the right life partner.

CHAPTER ONE

The Concept of Marriage.

As we all know, marriage is the union between a man and a woman to become husband and wife. God instituted marriage. In ***(Genesis 2:22-24 KJV) "And the rib, which the Lord God had taken from man, made he a woman, and brought her unto the man. And Adam said, this is now bone of my bones, and flesh of my flesh: She shall be called woman, because she was taken out of man. Therefore, shall a man leave his father and his mother, and shall cleave unto his wife; and they shall be one flesh."*** Marriage was God's design for mankind. In God's original plan, a man was not supposed to be lonely, as seen in ***(Genesis 2:18 KJV) "And the Lord God said, it is not good that the man should be alone, I will make him an help meet for him."*** We must come to the understanding that marriage is a way out of the life of loneliness.

The Bible clarifies that a man shall leave his father and mother, and marriage should not be a forced affair. Respectively speaking, there are some cultures in our world today where the parents lure their children into marriage against their will. Adam recognized that the woman was the bone of his bones and the flesh of his flesh; it was a choice. God has given man the free will to choose when it comes to marriage.

Marriage is also a "Union", an agreement between both parties. For marriage to occur, there must be an agreement between a man and a woman to become one. When it comes to marriage, you don't enforce or impose it on someone. There must be a mutual agreement, and without an agreement, there will be no marriage.

A lot of people in our world today prioritize cohabitation rather than marriage. Cohabitation is living together and being involved in a sexual relationship without being married legally. In ***(Hebrews 13:4 KJV) "Marriage is honourable in all, and the bed Undefiled: but whoremongers and adulterers God will judge."*** Any sexual relationship outside marriage is against God's command. Sex in marriage is a covenant and an expression of intimacy that exists between the husband and wife. This should be practiced with only those who are legitimately married; otherwise, it will be an act of fornication and adultery. And there is an eternal punishment for fornicators and adulterers. God's view about marriage is that it should be honourable, and any act of fornication or adultery would become dishonour. Anyone who commits fornication or adultery violates the divine command of God.

The Bible said ***(1 Corinthians 6:18 KJV), "Flee fornication, every sin that a man doeth is without the body; but he that committed fornication sinneth against his own body."*** The Marriage bed is to be kept pure and undefiled. A sexual relationship between husband and wife should be reserved for married couples alone.

Marriage bed can be defiled by fornication, adultery, pornography, homosexuality, prostitution, lesbianism etc. Chastity is a virtue that we all must embrace. Sex is sacred and is only for the two joined together to become one flesh. We must learn to honour the word of God above everything in our lives. If the word of God says we should "flee", then we should obey. Anything other than that will attract the wrath of God.

The Bible tells us that marriage is between a man and a woman. Marriage is not between a man and an animal or between a man and a man. Marriage is not between a woman and a woman but between a man and a woman. We are in a world where many people marry anything: you will see a man getting married to his fellow man; this is against the standard of God. We must understand the concept of marriage from God's own perspective.

The Bible says, ***"He who finds a wife finds what is good and receives favor from the Lord." (Proverbs 18:22 NIV).*** The Bible did not say he is joined to his wife or who marries a wife. The Bible says, "He who finds a wife" there must be a finding. The concept of finding means responsibility. It is a man's responsibility to search for his wife, and it is a woman's responsibility to position herself. Remember that we are looking at the concept of marriage from kingdom perspective and not from a worldly standpoint. Marriage is not man's initiative but God's initiative.

Marriage will not be complete without the consent and blessings from the Father and the Mother. They should prepare the children for marriage and give their consent and blessings. God will not recognize any marriage without parental witnesses. And in the situation where the parents are not available, there must be delegated people to represent them. Parental consent and approval are very Paramount if they must have a Godly home. The parents are also responsible for raising (training) the girl to become a virtuous woman ready for marriage. Also, they must train the boy from becoming a naive young man to becoming a responsible man. Marriage is not between a boy and a girl but between a man and a woman. That is, they must have attained some level of maturity. The concept of "leaving your father and mother" talks about responsibility. It means taking responsibility for raising your own family. Leaving your father and mother means that you shouldn't depend on your parents financially, spiritually, etc.

Respectively speaking, whether you are a Pastor, a Bishop, an Apostle, a Businessman and woman, Captains of industries, politicians, Academicians etc. If your marriage is not working, then something is missing that needs to be given necessary attention. Marriage can also measure a man's success. To an extent, marriage determines how successful a man or woman can be.

CHAPTER TWO

The Purpose of Marriage

There are reasons why God instituted marriage. God created everything to fulfill a purpose, including man. It is man's responsibility to find out the purpose God created a lot of things around him, and one of them is marriage. Marriage was enacted by God to fulfill God's purpose. It is wisdom to find out the purpose of marriage before going into it. The truth is that misuse is bound to occur due to ignorance of the use case of anything. This is one of the reasons why many are having issues in their Marriages today. Until you understand the purpose God instituted marriage, you cannot enjoy your union to the fullest. Below are five (5) primary purposes why God instituted marriage.

THE PURPOSE OF MARRIAGE.

1. Conforming to the Image of Christ.

The first reason God created man was for man to be like him and have his likeness. In ***(Genesis 1:26-27 KJV)*** ***"And God said, let us make man in our image, after our likeness: and let them have dominion over the fishes of the sea, and over the fowl of the air and over the cattle, and over all the earth, and over every creeping thing that creepeth upon the earth. So God Created man in his own image. In the image of God created he him; male and female created he them."*** So every marriage is supposed to mirror the image of God. We are to be like God because we were made in his image and likeness. In ***(Romans 8:29 KJV) "For whom he did foreknow, he also did predestinate to be conformed to the image of his son, that he might be the firstborn among many brethren."***

What God had concerning man was for man to conform to his Son Jesus Christ. What God expects in marriage is that the couple become like Christ. It is the responsibility of the man to shape the woman until she becomes like Christ, and it is also the woman's responsibility to shape the man until he becomes like Christ, they are both expected to reveal Christ to each other and together to the world. The extent of spiritual growth and transformation of the woman until she becomes like Christ is the man's responsibility. If he fails, God will ask him; the same also goes for the woman. The partners have been joined together as one, and it is their responsibility to watch and guide one another until they become like Christ. The reason for being joined together is for them to be nurtured to conform to the image of Christ. To be like Christ, think like Christ, and behave like Christ. If you are married and you are not conforming to the image of Christ, then you are not fulfilling God's purpose for marriage. If you are married and Christ is not revealed in your marriage, you have to go back to God for redirection. Your marriage must be conformed to the image of Christ otherwise, God's purpose for marriage would be defeated.

2. To Create a System of Oneness.

(Ephesians 5:31 KJV) "For this cause shall a man leave his father and mother, and shall be joined unto his wife, and they two shall be one flesh." The second purpose of marriage is to create a system of oneness. This is the system that exists among the Godhead (Trinity). God designed marriage for man and woman to coexist as one. The scripture above tells us that "*the two shall be one flesh,*" meaning two different beings coming together as one. God instituted marriage so that man would understand the mystery of oneness. No wonder the Bible says in ***(Mark 3:24 KJV) "If a Kingdom is divided against itself, that kingdom cannot stand."*** God is all Powerful and will always remain powerful not just because he is God alone, but because there is power and authority derived from oneness of the Trinity. That is how God designed marriage to be.

What happens when there is oneness in marriage?

a. They become a powerful force

(Genesis 11:1-9 KJV) "And the whole earth was of one language, and of one speech. And it came to pass, as they journeyed from the east, that they found a plain in the land of Shinar; and they dwelt there. And they said one to another, go to, let us make brick, and burn them thoroughly. And they had brick for stone, and slime had they for morter. And they said, go to, let us build us a city and a tower, whose top may reach unto heaven; and let

us make us a name, lest we be scattered abroad upon the face of the whole earth. And the Lord came down to see the city and the tower, which the children of men builded. And the Lord said, Behold, the people is one, and they have all one language; and this they begin to do: and now nothing will be restrained from them, which they have imagined to do. Go to, let us go down, and there confound their language, that they may not understand one another's speech. So the Lord scattered them abroad from thence upon the face of all the earth: and they left off to build the city. Therefore, is the name of it called Babel; because the Lord did there confound the language of all the earth: and from thence did the Lord scatter them abroad upon the face of all the earth." When they began to build the tower of Babel, God looked from heaven and said that the people were one and nothing they imagined to do could be stopped, so the only way God stopped them was to divide them. Anytime there is oneness in marriage, the couple becomes a powerful force. Satan cannot do anything wherever there is the oneness of the heart. No wonder the Bible tells us that a House divided against itself cannot stand. Any house with unity and oneness will be impossible for the devil to carry out his satanic operations. The Bible also said in ***(Matthew 18:19) " Again I say unto you that if two of you shall agree on Earth as touching anything that they shall ask, it shall be done for them for my father which is in heaven."*** One of the most incredible powers on earth is unity. When two becomes one, they become a potent force.

b. They attract divine attention.

When God saw that the children of Israel who were building the tower of Babel had become one, God came down. Anywhere there is unity and oneness, it attracts the presence of God. In ***(Matthew 18:20 KJV) "For where two or three are gathered together in my name, there am I in the midst of them."*** When a man and a woman are joined together in holy matrimony, Christ is also there in their midst. Unity attracts divine attention, and disunity invites satanic presence. Satan is always moving to and fro to sow the seed of disunity because that is where he can carry out his satanic activities. In case you are reading this book and your marriage is at the devil's mercy because of the seed of disunity sown, it is time to be intentional and reunite with your spouse. God will not dwell in a home that is not united; He only tabernacle in a home where there is oneness because that is his purpose for instituting marriage.

c. They become unbreakable, unmovable, and untouchable.

One thing that happens when there is oneness is that they become too strong to break. There is a force couple generate from the oneness that even the devil cannot break them. In ***(Deuteronomy 32:30 KJV) "How should one chase a thousand, and two put ten thousand to flight,***

except their Rock had sold them, and the Lord had shut them up?" The Bible says one will chase a thousand, and two will chase ten thousand. The ordinary arithmetic should be that two should Chase two thousand since one is chasing a thousand. It is an indication that oneness in marriage is very powerful, and it is impossible to break if they remain united. When a man and a woman are joined together in marriage, it becomes difficult and impossible to break their union. In marriage, the partners become unmovable and untouchable due to their oneness.

d. They enjoy divine favour.

(Proverbs 18:22 KJV) "Whosoever findeth a wife findeth a good thing, and obtaineth favour of the Lord." That means there is a dimension of God's favour you won't enjoy until you are married. There are divine blessings attached to marriage, and until you are married, you can't be a benefactor. When a man and a woman are joined together as husband and wife, they enjoy a dimension of God's favour that singles can't experience. There are some blessings God has reserved exclusively for marriage, and until you are married, you can't be a partaker.

3. Fellowship and Companionship.

(Genesis 2:18 KJV) "And the Lord said, it is not good that the man should be alone; I will make him a help meet for him." One of the primary aims why God instituted marriage was to erase loneliness. The scripture above says that, "*and God said that it is not good for a* *man to be alone."* God instituted marriage for fellowship and companionship. According to God's organogram for marriage, it is expedient for a man and a woman to come together to fellowship with one another. The idea of marriage is for a man and a woman to be dependent on each other. God knew that it wouldn't be suitable for a man to spend all his life on earth alone, so he brought a woman to compliment him. Marriage is a platform where a man and a woman complete each other.

In our society today, a lot of people have neglected the concept of companionship in marriage. The couple is to enjoy friendship and cordial relationship with each other. Many couples are suffering in marriage today not because they didn't meet marriage requirements but because they are neglecting the concepts of companionship and fellowship. Marriage is not just for procreation alone but for friendship, fellowship, and companionship. As a couple, if you are not completing or fellowshipping with one another, you are violating the purpose of marriage. As a husband, you are meant to build a friendship with your wife and spend time with each other. When God created the woman, it was the man that recognized that she was the bone of his bones and flesh of his flesh. So as a husband or potential husband, you must acknowledge that she is your companion. Both of you must spend time with each other and keeps each other company. Marriage will be boring without building a friendship with your partner and keeping each other's company. There must be an agreement and acceptance between the couple. ***(Amos 3:3 KJV) "Can two walk together except they be agreed?"*** Couples must learn to grow and build a friendship with each other.

In ***(Ecclesiastes 4:9-11 KJV) "Two are better than one; because they have a good reward for their labour. For if they fall, the one will lift up his fellow: but woe to him that is alone when he falleth; for he hath not another to help him up. Again, if two lie together, then they have heat: but how can one be warm alone?"*** Marriage is a long journey; that's why God has provided you with a companion, someone you can share your joy with, someone you can share your pains with, someone who can bear the burdens with you, someone you can share your challenges with. It becomes unfair not to spend time with your spouse; it's unfair not to give him or her attention. Some people are married but are still lonely because there is no connection between the couple. That is why it is imperative to marry your friend. There is a friend that sticks closer than a brother. Friendship is essential in marriage, and it is one of the pillars that holds marriage. I have seen in many marriages today where the couple isolates themselves. They don't talk and discuss with each other. No man is an Island. Therefore, couples must build friendship and fellowship together. Any home where there is no friendship between the pair cannot stand. Marriage will be a boring place without friendship and companionship. When God created Adam, he put him in charge of everything he made, but God saw that the man needed a companion, so he created the woman to be a help meet for him, support him, and erase loneliness from him. Friendship, companionship, and fellowship are one of the purposes God instituted marriage.

4. Procreation (Raising Godly Seed).

In ***(Genesis 1:28 KJV) "And God blessed them, and God said unto them, be fruitful, and multiply, and replenish the earth and subdue it: and have dominion over the fish of the sea, and over the fowl of the air, and over every living thing that moveth upon the earth."*** God's first command was "be fruitful". The very nature of God is to multiply life on earth, while the character of Satan is to multiply death upon the earth. Procreation was part of God's original plan and designed for marriage. Raising Children will help you understand God better. God didn't create man to remain alone but build a home and raise godly children. No wonder God blessed them and commanded them to be fruitful, which means to bear fruits and multiply, meaning to be productive on earth.

In ***(Malachi 2:15 KJV) "And did not he make one? Yet had he the residue of the spirit. And wherefore one? That he might seek a godly seed. Therefore, take heed to your spirit, and let none deal treacherously against the wife of his youth."*** The Bible talks about raising godly Seed. That is why when you are a believer; you must also marry a believer because it is when both of you are godly before you can raise a godly Seed. ***(2 Corinthians 6:14 KJV). "Be ye not unequally yoked together with unbelievers: for what fellowship hath righteousness with unrighteousness? And what communion hath light with darkness?"*** The Bible clearly stated that we should not be unequally yoked with an unbeliever. When you marry an unbeliever, you cannot fulfill the purpose of raising a godly Seed. God wants two believers to come together to raise children in His ways. This is not all about giving birth to children but raising, nurturing, and training them in the way of the Lord. Your children should be able to learn and emulate your lifestyle as a couple. God instituted marriage as a platform where children are nurtured to fulfill their destiny. Couples should be able to live and show the children the right way of living by their character because children learn more from what they see than what they hear. Procreation and Raising Godly Seed is one of the purposes God instituted marriage.

5. Sexual Intimacy and commitment.

(1 Corinthians 7:2-5 KJV) "Nevertheless, to avoid fornication, let every man have his own wife, and let every woman have her own husband. Let the husband render unto the wife due benevolence: and likewise also the wife unto the husband. The wife hath not power of her own body, but the husband: and likewise also the husband hath not power of his own body, but the wife. Defraud ye not one the other, except it be with consent for a time, that ye may give yourselves to fasting and

prayer; and come together again that Satan tempt ye not for your incontinency." Sex is potent and highly spiritual. It is beyond the emotions and physical ecstasy; it is highly spiritual. It has a spiritual connection and intimacy. Sex is good and enjoyable only when married, and it should only be practiced between married couples. God created us naked and unashamed and planted in us sexual desire. Moreover, that desire is to be managed and controlled until when married.

In the scripture we read above, Paul admonished that it is paramount for every man to have his own wife and for every woman to have her own husband to avoid fornication. The rate of fornication in our world today is alarming, and it is against the commandments of God. In Verse 9 of the above scripture, Paul warned that you should marry if you cannot hold yourself.

Sexual intimacy and commitment are one of the purposes of marriage. Sex in marriage makes a man and a woman more intimate and committed to each other. As a married couple, your spouse has the right to your body. The Bible says that couples shouldn't defraud one another; don't deprive your spouse of sex. Sex is vital in marriage because it brings unity and oneness in marriage. Sex is not for the singles or the unmarried but the married. That you are engaged or preparing for marriage is not a yardstick for involvement in sexual act, it is exclusively for the married. Sex binds couples together spiritually, psychologically, physically, and emotionally. So, Sexual intimacy and commitments are one of the purposes God instituted marriage.

CHAPTER THREE

Qualities You Should Look Out for in a Man.

There are numerous qualities a man ought to have, but here are some excellent qualities a man should possess before considering him to be Man. Ladies, you must find these qualities below in a man before saying yes to him.

1. A Man that Fears God.

(Proverbs 1:7 KJV) "The fear of the Lord is the beginning of knowledge: but fools despise wisdom and instruction." The fear of the Lord has been misunderstood in our world today. Societies have defined fear of God to be just believing in God. There is a discrepancy between fear of God and believing in God. Someone can believe in God and yet doesn't fear him. The fear of the Lord has to do with submitting to the leadership of God and obeying all his instructions. The fear of God has to do with submitting to God in everything. Unfortunately, some men are born again but don't submit to God in all things. And it is one of the reasons why many men maltreat their wives and still feel okay to do so. To be God-fearing means to have respect and honor for God. So many men believe that God exists but doesn't have respect and reverence for him. Respecting God has to do with obeying him wholly and timely. A man that fears God must submit to God as the final head in all things. We are in a world where many men want their opinions and decisions to be final in every matter. We must realize that the word of God must be the final authority in all things. Culture and traditions should not be the final authority in your home but the word of God.

When a man fears God, he will never raise his hands to hit his wife. The Bible says that man should love his wife just like Christ loved the church. So if a man sees the word of God as the final authority, he will never disobey God by violating the commands of God. Many men do not fear God. A man that does not fear God cannot raise a family to fear God. A man that fears God will raise his children to respect and honor God. Before saying yes to him, a man's most important quality in a man who loves and fears God genuinely. Please do not say yes to him, hoping that you will change him when you are married; you are not the Holy Spirit. He must be genuinely born again and fear God before you accept him, irrespective of his academic qualifications and financial achievements.

The most important thing to look out for when a man approaches you is not his pockets, cars, or even houses but his love for God and his relationship with God. Having a fear of God doesn't necessarily mean praying for 12 hours daily or speaking in tongues, but having a fear of the Lord means submitting to the authority of the word of God in everything. Ladies, hear me, the greatest mistake you can make in marriage is to marry a man who doesn't fear God.

God-fearing is not all about being a church goer or doing activities in the church. It is not even the position held in the church that determines whether a man fears God or not but having respect and reverence for God and submitting to him as the final authority. Being a Pastor is not even a yardstick to know if a man fears God because, respectfully speaking, many pastors today don't fear God. So, ladies, you must ensure he is a God-fearing man before saying yes to him.

2. A Man Who Has Vision.

(Habakkuk 2:2 KJV) "And the Lord answered me, and said, write the vision, and make it plain upon tables, that he may run that readeth it." One of the vital qualities you must find in a man before accepting him is that he must be visionary. A man who is preparing for an extraordinary life must have a vision. By vision, I mean your future plans. What are your goals, and what strategies have you put in place? What do you want to become, and how are you working towards achieving it? For a man to be visionary, he must have life goals and dreams.

Being visionary or having goals is very important because it shows that he is not complacent. There are questions you can ask a man to know if he is a visionary or not. What career does he want to build? What are his financial plans? Does he embrace God's leadership in his life? Is he disciplined to bring those plans to reality? These are essential questions to know if he is a visionary because many men are not visionary. Some men are Lazy and dependent. Some men want to marry but still depend on parental assistance. A visionary man always has plans and goals with the necessary strategies to actualize those dreams. After asking him those questions, listen to how he talks about those topics.

In ***(Proverbs 29:18 KJV) "Where there is no vision, the people perish: but he that keepeth the law, happy is he."*** A man with no vision is going nowhere. As a man, you must have plans for your life because a man without plans will be an irresponsible husband and father. Set life goals that you intend to achieve in the nearest future and work towards actualizing those plans. Do not marry a man who has no vision, plans and going nowhere because there are possibilities that the marriage will be a disaster.

3. A man who loves, cares, and has a genuine passion for you.

(Ephesians 5:28-29 KJV) "*So ought men to love their wives as their bodies. He that loveth his wife loveth himself. For no man ever get hated his own flesh; but nourisheth and cherisheth it, even as the Lord the church.*" Never marry a man who doesn't understand the Biblical concept of love. The Bible is a manual that leads to a successful marriage. Many married men have issues with their spouses because they have not understood the concept of love from a Kingdom perspective. The Bible clearly states that men should love their wives as their bodies. A man cannot hate his own body, so he shouldn't hate his wife either; just like how a man nourishes his body and takes care of it, the same should apply to his wife. It is God's design for a man to take care of his wife, supply for her needs, support her and spend time with her. I have seen many marriages where the man doesn't demonstrate love to his wife, doesn't care about his wife, doesn't spend time with her, and doesn't support her in any way. This is one of the primary reasons why many struggles in their marriages today. So what you should look out for in a man is a man who loves, care, and has a genuine passion for his partner. It begins in relationship and courtship, and if a man is showing this in a relationship and courtship, then in marriage, he will also display it.

A man who does not have a genuine passion and love for his partner can easily cheat on her. In any marriage with no passion, there are tendencies that there will be unfaithfulness. Passion is a resolve within you that through your partner you have satisfaction. She must not even be the most educated or beautiful, but it is a resolve within you that you derived utmost satisfaction and fulfillment through her. Many wives feel insecure today because their husbands are not passionate about them.

(Ephesians 5:28-29) Where we read, the Bible clearly states that husbands should love their wives just like Christ loved the church; for a man to understand the Biblical concept of love, he needs to know how Christ loved the church. Christ loved the church to the extent that he died for us even when we were sinners. Even when the church isn't perfect and undeserving of his love, he still loves the church. He sacrificed himself for the church. As a man, you must understand that you can sacrifice anything for her when you say you love her. When you say you love her, you will inconvenience yourself for her. Some men can verbally claim that they love their partners, but they cannot sacrifice their time and resources for the lady. Any man who cannot sacrifice for his partner doesn't love her. You profess love to her, and you cannot inconvenience yourself for her; that love is not complete. Because of his love for the church, Jesus Christ, who is God, He inconvenienced himself and came to the earth to demonstrate his love for man. Ladies, marry a man who loves you, cares about you, and has a genuine passion for you.

4. A Man that is Responsible and diligent.

Many men in our world today are irresponsible and lazy. Some are spiritual and tongue talking brothers but are not responsible. To be responsible means to be accountable for action and its consequences. It can also mean taking cognizance of the cost dimension of life. It is the awareness that something needs to be done. We are in a world today where many young men are irresponsible, including older men, due to where they are coming from. You will see a young man of 25-30 years idle, doing nothing because he has been over pampered. As a result of this over pampering from his parents, he will grow up and get married and become irresponsible. Some families are the reasons why many men today are irresponsible. Many irresponsible men expect to be a recipient and not contributors. They are indolent and prefer to sit and expect everything to be done. Most of them might be born again and tongue talking brothers, but they don't want anything that will discomfort them. Irresponsibility is the reason we have many lazy men all around the world today.

God's word clarifies that we are instructed to work hard and put our best effort into doing something. Laziness has no place in the character of a follower of Jesus. In ***(Genesis 2:15 KJV) "The Lord God took the man and put him in the Garden of Eden to work it and take care of it."*** God didn't create man to be irresponsible and idle. He created man to work and be responsible. In **(Proverbs 10:5 KJV)** ***"He that gathereth in summer is a wise son: but he that sleepeth in harvest is a son that causeth shame."*** God doesn't and will never encourage laziness and irresponsibility. Any man who is not diligent and hard-working is a disgraceful son. ***(Proverbs 14:23 NIV) "All hardwork brings a profit, but mere talk leads only to poverty."*** A lazy man will not feed his family because he will use crises in the world as an excuse. A lazy man will not sow because there is cold, and he will also not reap. As a man who wants to be responsible, you must learn to be an initiator and not just a recipient. There are so many married men today who sit and fold their hands and expect salaries from their wives to sustain the family; it is okay if he loses his job temporarily and in the case of health condition. Aside from these reasons, it is unfair as a man to sit at home doing nothing and expect the woman to sustain the family.

(Proverbs 10:4 KJV) "He becometh poor that dealeth with a slack hand: but the hand of the diligent maketh rich." Regardless of his current status, every diligent man becomes rich and wealthy due to consistent hard work. It doesn't matter how he started, but as long as he has the quality of diligence, he actualises his dreams and goals at the end of the day. A diligent and responsible man is a hard-working and industrious man. He is someone who will carry out a task and do it effectively and efficiently. Ladies hear me; as long as the man you are planning to marry is responsible and diligent, he will take care of you and your children. He will also provide for the basic needs of the family. But suppose the man you plan to marry is irresponsible and not diligent. In that case, it is obvious that your marriage will be disastrous because the children's school fees won't be paid, medical bills and the family's basic needs won't be carter for. When you marry a lazy and irresponsible man, you won't be happy and comfortable in your marriage.

How will you know if a man is diligent and responsible? A diligent and responsible man, every assignment and task given to him, he will do it effectively and efficiently. He will always bring results from everything he does, no matter the difficulties of the job. When a man takes care of his responsibilities, the task and assignments given to him, whether at his workplace, church or even at home, he can produce a result. Then that person is responsible and diligent. A diligent and responsible man sets goals and targets, and he is able to achieve the goals and targets. Being responsible is not all about having a car and a house because that's the indices most ladies are using to measure whether a man is responsible or not. A man can have a car and a house by association. Before saying yes to any man, make sure he is responsible and diligent.

5. A Man Who Has a Father Figure.

The fifth quality to look out for in a man before marriage is that the man must have a father figure in his life. Someone who gives him instructions and he obeys, someone he listens to. If you marry a man who has no father figure in his life, he will treat you like a slave and can do anything to you without anyone saying anything to him. A father figure is someone who has gone ahead of you spiritually and otherwise, who speaks and you listen to. The essence of a father figure is to lead, direct, correct and show you the right path. One of the reasons why many marriages are failing today is because the man doesn't have a father figure in his life, so he can hit his wife whenever he feels like it. He can maltreat the woman because no one can speak to him that he listens.

Ladies, before marrying a man, he must be able to submit to an earthly authority for building, correcting, nurturing, training and mentorship. Never marry a man who does not have a father figure, a mentor and a pastor in his life to listen to and obey. Some men don't want to submit to anyone because they don't want anybody to correct and tell them what to do. Part of the reason many men are unfaithful in marriages today is that they don't have a father figure in their lives. They can go and have an extramarital affair, and the wife cannot talk to him because when she speaks to him, he will hit her. Any man that doesn't have an earthly authority might not be faithful to his wife. Before you marry him, make sure you are confident that he has a father figure in his life that he listens to. You should look out for numerous qualities in a man, but the five qualities listed above are essential in choosing your husband.

CHAPTER FOUR

Qualities You Should Look Out for in a Woman.

There are a lot of qualities a lady should possess before marrying her. Men, the followings are the things you must find in a lady before proposing to her.

1. A Woman who is genuinely born again and fears God.

(Proverbs 31:30 KJV) "Favour is deceitful, and beauty is vain: but a woman that feareth the Lord, she shall be praised." Men, never you marry a woman who does not fear God genuinely and wholeheartedly. A woman who does not love and fear God can easily be unfaithful. A woman who fear God is a woman who respect God at all times. A woman who fear God is someone who submits to God as the final authority in all things. Many ladies are unfaithful in their marriages today because they don't fear God. They don't see extramarital affairs as a big deal. They can commit adultery without feeling any guilt.

Men, the most important quality you should look out for in a woman is a woman who fears the Lord. Lack of fear of the Lord is one of the reasons many marriages are failing today. A woman is a homemaker and a home builder, and any not God-fearing lady cannot raise God-fearing children. You cannot teach what you are not; a woman who is not born again cannot build a godly home. The scripture above tells us that beauty does not last, but a woman who fears the Lord shall be praised, just paraphrasing. Men listen carefully; when choosing a woman, you want to spend the rest of your life with, make sure she has this quality. A woman that fears the Lord will not look down on her husband. One of the most outstanding qualities a woman can have is fear and reverence for God. There are many qualities a woman possesses, but this is the most essential of them.

2. A Woman Who is Submissive in Everything.

(Ephesians 5:22-24 KJV) "Wives, Submit yourselves unto your own husbands, as unto the Lord. For the husband is the head of the wife, even as Christ is the head of the Church: and he is the Saviour of the body. Therefore, as the church is subject unto Christ, so let the wives be to their own husbands in everything." The word of the Lord is the manual for a glorious marriage. The Bible clearly states that a wife should submit to her husband at all times. As a potential wife, you must understand that submission is not a thing of choice. Submission shouldn't be a problem if you must experience a glorious marriage. Submission is not weakness; it is the ability to bring your strength under control. Those who submit are not weak people; they are the mature ones.

The Bible made us understand that wives should submit in everything and not in some things. We are in a world where many women submit in some things; incomplete submission is not submission. What is demanded of you is absolute submission. Your submission shouldn't be conditional. You submit to him only when he brings money to the house and fulfils his responsibilities, that is submission with conditions. But the Bible says wives should submit in everything. I understand that submission is not easy; you need God to help you. Many ladies don't submit to their partners because they do not provide anything; if you do that, you disobey God's instructions. Remember that it is when your obedience is complete before you can judge someone's disobedience. Submission can sometimes be challenging because there are times when your submission and loyalty will be tested. Many will mock you, but you must decide to obey God in everything.

We are in a world where many ladies mistake submission to be a weakness. Submission is not a weakness and foolishness as some think but maturity. Submission starts from your relationship; it is not when you are married that you practice how to submit. It must begin with your relationship. Submission is not all about human worship; it is bringing your strength and everything under control. Men, before proposing to her, does she submit at all times?

3. A Woman who Honours and Respects her partner.

(Ephesians 5:33 NIV) "However, each one of you also must love his wife as he love himself, and the wife must

respect her husband." God made the husband the head of the wife and instructed the wife to respect and honour him. The husband being the head of the family doesn't necessarily mean that the wife is less important, but it simply means that the husband has been given the leadership role in the marriage in God's eye. As a good and virtuous lady, you must recognize the man's leadership and respect him. Men, never you marry a Lady who doesn't respect you because any lady that won't respect you won't respect your parents and everyone around you.

Ladies, hear me, respect and honour is not foolishness and human worship but maturity. In Ephesians 5:33, where we read above, implies that wives need love and husbands need respect. It means that the husband must love his wife even if the wife doesn't respect him, and the wife must respect her husband even if her husband doesn't love her. So a husband is commanded by God to love his disrespectful wife, and the wife is instructed to respect her unloving husband. We are in a world where many women will say that they will respect their husbands if only he loves them. The respect you should have for your husband should be unconditional, irrespective of who he is and what he has done. Respect and honour are the love language of men. Ladies, the best way to communicate love to your husband is to honour and respect him. If you must experience a successful relationship and marriage, you must learn to respect and honour your partner. Love to a man is respect and honour, so don't marry a lady who does not respect and honour you; otherwise, your marriage will be in jeopardy.

4. A woman who is sacrificial and hospitable.

(1 Peter 4:8-10 NIV) "Above all, love each other deeply, because love covers over a multitude of sin. Offer hospitality to one another without grumbling." A sacrificial woman is one who can inconvenience herself for the growth and comfort of her home. A woman who is not sacrificial cannot make a good wife and a good mother. A sacrificial woman is someone who can forgo many things for the development and growth of her home. Men, never marry a lady who cannot sacrifice because your home will sadly be a disaster. A woman should be able to sacrifice her time, energy and strength, and even her resources for the growth of her home.

The scripture above clearly commands and instructs us to show hospitality to one another without grumbling. Many ladies in our world are not hospitable. ***(Matthew 25:40 NIV) "The King will reply, 'Truly I tell you, whatever you did for one of the least of these brothers and sisters of mine, you did for me."*** Like many people welcome Jesus in their homes with open arms, we should do likewise. When we serve others, we are saving others. Hospitality is not only your household but the state of your heart. Hospitality is receiving and welcoming people; it is giving freely to others. People can easily forget what you said, forget what you did. But people will never forget how you made them feel. Only a life lived to the service of others is worth living. Many women don't know how to welcome in-laws and visitors into their homes. Many marriages are failing today because the ladies are not sacrificial and hospitable. As a potential wife, you must learn to inconvenience yourself for others and receive and welcome people warmly.

5. A woman who is physically attractive.

(Song of Songs 1:15 NIV) "How beautiful you are, my darling! Oh, how beautiful! Your eyes are doves" The physical aspect is not the most important factor because they can fade like a leaf; however, the physical aspect is still important. I will only advise the men not to focus on the physical factor alone because they cannot sustain relationships and marriage. Still, they can assist other qualities in helping sustain a home. Brothers, I am not saying the physical quality is not essential, but it will become a problem when you focus on the physical quality above the four qualities I have listed beforehand. I am emphasizing this because this is where many men missed it. They focus on the physical beauty alone.

Nevertheless, the woman should be physically attracted to her partner. I am not talking about seduction and being nude. I am talking about taking care of your body, looking good, dressing well, and being physically okay. Many ladies are spiritual but don't pay attention to their bodies;

they dress anyhow, and some even have bad body odor. As a woman, you should be physically attracted to your husband because if you are not attractive to him, another lady will be. As a lady preparing for marriage, you must learn to look bright and beautiful. Stop indecent dressing, thinking that it doesn't matter; it really matters. Don't dress because you want to impress your partner; instead, let it be a lifestyle. Use good perfume, good soap and body cream to make you look good. If you can't afford the expensive ones, go for the ones you can afford and look decent and attractive to your partner.

Also, as a lady preparing for marriage, you must learn to keep your home clean and tidy at all times. Keep all parts of the home neat, especially your toilet, kitchen, and living room. Any dirty woman won't make a good wife. Your environment and furniture must be kept clean at all times. Many women don't pay attention to cleanliness; it is not a good character. There are some homes that a visitor will enter and will never wish to visit again because of the level of disorderliness and uncleanliness. Ladies, if you are preparing for marriage, you must take cognizance of all these things. Wash your clothes when dirty, including bed sheets, blankets, and body towels. No man will want to marry a dirty lady. You must be neat and physically attractive. There are many qualities a woman should possess, but the five mentioned above are very Paramount.

CHAPTER FIVE

Reasons why marriages fail.

Marriages fail for different reasons, and any of the issues highlighted here should give cause for concern and Care. If you wonder why your relationship and marriage are failing, then this list may have the answers. Below are some of the reasons why many marriages fail:

1. Spiritual Incompatibility.

This is a situation where both couple doesn't connect spiritually. That is, they don't share the same spiritual beliefs. ***(2 Corinthians 6:14-16 KJV). "Be ye not Unequally yoked together with unbelievers: For what fellowship hath righteousness with unrighteousness? And what communion hath light with darkness? And what Concord hath Christ with Belial? Or what part hath he that believeth with an infidel? And what agreement hath the temple of God with idols? For ye are the temple of the living God; as God hath said, I will dwell in them, and walk in them: and I will be their God, and they shall be my people".*** The scripture clearly emphasized that we should not be unequally yoked. This has been the major problem in marriages today; it will definitely become a problem when you marry a partner who doesn't share the same faith with you. For instance, when a believer marries an unbeliever, both of them will never be compatible when it comes to spiritual matters. I have seen in some marriages where the wife will come to church alone because the husband doesn't believe in going to church. Sadly, this has resulted in conflicts and failures in marriages in our world today. What becomes the children's faith when a believing wife marries an unbelieving husband? Do they follow the steps of their father or mother? So this has been a major problem in marriages that have caused marriage failure.

The likelihood that two people will be successful together in a relationship or marriage is predicated on their ability to find common ground on many things. One of them is spiritual compatibility. If you ever wonder why couples break up for irreconcilable differences, then this is one. Their mindset and ideologies of how things should work in marriage must have become unworkably disconnected and detached. Spiritual incompatibility doesn't only talk about whether one partner is a believer or not. It also means that both partners have different ideologies and mindsets about spiritual matters. For instance, we have different denominations around the world with various doctrines. Let's say 'MR A' attend a denomination that doesn't believe in speaking in tongues, putting on trousers as a lady etc. and 'MR B' attend a denomination that supports and believe these things. There will be conflict of ideologies, which will definitely lead to marriage failure.

What is my counsel? Both of you must subject your different ideologies to the word of God. The word of the Lord God is the Manual for our lives and must be obeyed at all times and in every matter.

2. Infidelity.

This is the act of being unfaithful to your partner. It is engaging in sexual or romantic relationships with a person other than your partner. It's the second reason why marriages fail. For instance, when a man cheats on his wife or has extramarital affairs, it can lead to marriage failure or divorce. It takes Commitment, integrity and discipline not to lust after a person. When you don't have all these armour, you won't be able to stand the temptation of being unfaithful in your marriage.

We live in a world where many have become addicted to extramarital affairs. You will see a perfect and beautiful couple, yet one partner will derive happiness in having an affair outside his or her marriage. This thing is a spirit and must be well managed and controlled; otherwise, it will wreck many homes. Negligence and carelessness are also some of the causes of infidelity in marriage.

What is my Counsel? You must remain prayerful, committed to your partner, focused and disciplined. When you practice these genuinely, then you will experience a glorious marriage.

3. Lack of Quality Time and Attention.

Time is what we all need in life. It takes time to grow, be in love and marry. Time is one of the most precious things that every human being need. One of the problems experienced in relationships and marriages today is a lack of quality time and attention. There are so many marriages where the partners don't often talk and don't spend time together. Some even use the nature of their job and businesses as an excuse. Note this; No relationship or marriage will succeed without the investment of time. For a marriage to work or be successful, you must invest your time in it.

Whatever you love, you create out time for. If you love God, you must have time for him, and if you genuinely love your partner, you must create time for him or her. As a couple, when you don't pay attention to your partner, you don't spend time with him or her, it will certainly cause marriage failure. When a partner spends his or her time outside their marriage, there are possibilities that the marriage will suffer. I have seen in most marriages where both partners are preoccupied with too many activities that take them away from home early in the morning and return late at night. If this happens over a long time, it is a concern and will possibly lead to marriage failure and divorce in most cases.

What is my counsel? Couples must ensure they create out time despite their busy schedules and must pay careful attention to each other's needs and emotions.

4. Issues of Sex.

Research over the years regarding the cause of failed marriage suggests that sex alone cannot sustain marriage even though it is essential in marriages. Sex is an emotional bond. That is, it has the ability to bring couples closer and very intimate. One of the most pressing challenges in marriage is the issue of sex. There are different issues surrounding sex, for instance, the inability to satisfy your partner sexually. Sex is for the enjoyment and satisfaction of both parties. In a situation whereby one party is not satisfied, it might possibly result in an issue in marriage. Many people don't consider the satisfaction of his or her partner; this is selfishness. Also another issue surrounding sex is sex starvation. I have heard in some marriages where a partner is starved of sex. It is a high level of selfishness to have sex only when you are in the mood. What happens when your partner is in the mood, and you are not?

As a couple, you must ensure that both of you are in the right mood, and in a situation whereby one party isn't in the mood, you have to put him or her in the right mood. This alone has wrecked many homes to pieces. You should also be considerate when it comes to sex, especially when your partner is exasperated and exhausted, probably because of the hectic day at work. Also, when he or she isn't feeling too well. Unsatisfied sexual life and not considering the partner's emotional state have led to marriage failures.

What is my counsel? For your marriage to work, both partners must be considerate and be on the same page regarding sex.

5. Financial Challenges.

Finance is essential in marriage. The man, in most cases, bears the financial burden of the family. In a scenario where the man can no longer meet the family's financial demands, it could become a problem. There are so many people who may not be patient enough for a long time in the midst of lack and penury. Money might not be everything, but it can strengthen your relationship and marriage. Also, in a situation where the wife cannot support the family financially, it can result in a problem in marriage. The issue of finance has led to fights and conflicts in homes today. Financial issues in a marriage that is not well managed can easily result in resentment and distress at home. It can also affect the growth process of children due to financial limitations because school fees won't be paid, and other basic needs of the children won't be provided due to financial constraints.

Some couples are debating who should provide and bring money to the family; that is why it is imperative to understand your role in the marriage. And the couple needs to sort out things like this during their courtship and engagement period. Questions like, who should be the chief financial burden-bearer? Roles of both parties as regards the issue of finance. This has been one of the reasons why many partners have failed in their responsibilities. Couples must define their financial role well. These financial issues have caused marriage failures.

What is my counsel? Couples must define their financial role very well from the onset. Also, you must learn to support your partner financially.

CHAPTER SIX

Keys to Sustain your Relationship and Marriage.

Every marriage is the foundation of a family. And family is one of the most important units of a society. Without a successful and healthy marriage, families might be in a disaster. Children might become failures, and the world might not be a conducive place to live in. This is why God Almighty has given us a Patten and standard on how husband and wife can build and maintain quality, successful, happy, and healthy relationships. The Followings are ways of keys to help you sustain and strengthen your relationship and marriage:

1. Praying Together.

(James 5:16 NIV) "Therefore confess your sins to each other and pray for each other so that you may be healed. The prayer of a righteous person is powerful and effective." The Bible encourage us to pray for one another. This is actually an excellent activity that will help your marriage to succeed. Prayer is vital and necessary in life; we cannot succeed without prayers as believers. **(Luke 18:1 KJV)** ***"And he spake a parable unto them to this end, that men ought always to pray, and not to faint."*** Jesus said that men ought always to pray and not faint. It means prayer is a necessity if you must sustain your marriage.

When you pray together, it strengthens your relationship with your partner. The Bible says when two of you agree on anything in His name (Jesus), it shall be done; just paraphrasing. So when couples pray together, it brings a speedy response. It also generates power. When couples pray together, they become too powerful that the devil cannot break their bond. You must cultivate the habit of praying for your spouse. Wife, pray for your husband, and the husband must also learn to pray for his wife. By doing so, their relationship and marriage become strengthened. There are occasions that sometimes you might be weak and exhausted, but it's in the prayer that you receive strength. Show me a praying couple, and I will show you an unbreakable couple. Prayer is one of the tools we can use to war against negative spiritual occurrences. Praying together is one of the most vital keys to sustaining your relationship and marriage.

2. Mutual Honour and Respect.

Respect in this context means having high regard and reverence for your partner. Respect is the way people treat what they value. If a thing is highly valued, a person will treat it with honour and dignity. Respect is one of the ingredients that sustain relationships and marriage. Thus, without respect in marriage, partners will feel devalued. ***(1 Peter 2:17 NIV) "Show proper respect to everyone, love***

the family of believers, fear God, honour the emperor." The Bible says we should show proper respect to everyone.

Also, honour must be two-sided. One-sided honour may not sustain your relationship and marriage, which is why honour must be mutual. One-sided honour will always create tension in relationships and marriage. For instance, when a husband honours his wife, whether privately or publicly, the wife must find a way to reciprocate that honour; otherwise, the honour will be one-sided. One-sided honour is not enough to sustain your marriage. Or, as a husband, every time your wife always appreciates you, tell people around her how good you are. It is not appropriate to just sit and enjoy the moment alone; you must also find a way of reciprocating the honour. Lack of honour has cost many their marriages; you must sincerely honour your spouse. Mutual respect and honour are significant ingredients to maintaining relationships and marriage. Honour must be two-sided, whether in a love relationship or marriage.

3. Effective Communication.

Communication is one of the bases of relationships and marriage. The fact that couples spend most of their time under one roof does not mean that they communicate effectively with one another. So, to sustain and maintain your relationship and marriage, it is essential to communicate effectively between couples. It's good you know what's happening in your partner's life, and if you don't know, you won't understand the issues they may be dealing with. When there is poor communication between couples, it would slowly lead to a lack of interest in each other's lives, and it can also strain your relationship and marriage. It is, therefore, paramount to have effective communication.

Couples who have effective communication have a better understanding of each other. Effective communication also helps couples to have a stronger bond with each other. When you understand your partner and the situation he or she is experiencing, there is lesser scope for ambiguity. Better communication means better satisfaction in a relationship and marriage, in which you share everything with each other, and it leads to lesser fights, conflicts and disagreements. Communication is also a way you express your feelings and emotions towards your partner. Being expressive and vocal is a vital way of exhibiting your feelings towards your partner, leading to a better connection between couples.

4. Value.

There is a popular saying that to be valued is to be given a feeling that you can't easily be replaced. If your relationship and marriage must work, you must provide your partner with a sense of value. Almost everyone won't be able to remain in a relationship when they are being devalued. Everyone on Earth wants to be valued. Every human being wants to feel loved, valued, appreciated and important. When these desires are not met, there will be tension in your relationship and even in marriage. I have seen in many marriages today where a spouse makes his or her partner feel less important, which has caused many problems in marriages today. Relationships and marriage won't work properly when both parties neglect the concept of value. If you must sustain your relationship and marriage, you must understand and communicate value to your partner. Give your partner the feeling that they are important and valued. Never give your partner a sense of replacing him or her, even when there are obvious weaknesses. Communicating value is not flattery; you must understand this. Anytime you talk with your partner, give him or her an idea that he or she is important.

To sustain your relationship and marriage, couples should communicate value to one another. Make your partner feel important, loved and appreciated. Most couples don't know how to appreciate one another. When your partner does anything for you, whether small or great, you must learn to appreciate him or her. When you appreciate your spouse, he or she will be motivated to do more. To maintain your relationship and marriage, you must learn to appreciate one another. Sometimes your partner doesn't necessarily have to do something for you before you appreciate him or her; you can appreciate him or her for being your partner and standing by you. Just learn to make him or her feel important. If you don't learn this as a couple, you will be surprised why your marriage is not working even if you love each other. To maintain your relationship and marriage, you must understand the concept of value and communicate it to your partner at all times.

5. Forgiving One another.

(Ephesians 4:32 NIV) ***"Be kind and compassionate to one another, forgiving each other, just as in Christ God forgave you."*** Forgiveness plays a vital role in marriages. Unforgivingness is the reason for resentment and bitterness in relationships and marriage. As a couple, you must cultivate the habit of forgiving one another no matter the gravity of the offence. When couples forgive each other at all times, they tend to have a happy and successful marriage.

Marriage begins to fail and fall apart when one partner holds a grudge in his or her heart. It would be best to try as quickly as possible to forgive your partner whenever they do anything wrong. Holding a grudge in your heart won't help you and your partner. You must also learn to sincerely apologize, admit your fault and ask for forgiveness whenever you wrong your partner. You must understand that as humans, we have a lot of weaknesses in us, so making mistakes is bound to happen. You must learn to forgive your partner even if you are badly hurt; this makes marriage interesting. Marriage is not for two perfect beings but two beings working towards perfection.

Just like Christ Forgave us, even when we didn't deserve his forgiveness, you must do likewise. This is one of the most important keys to sustaining your relationship and marriage.

CHAPTER SEVEN

How to Know When You Are Ready for Marriage.

There have been a lot of confusions and questions like; at what age should a man or a Lady get married? Am I ready for marriage when I graduate from an institution? Etc. I tell you that age does not necessarily determine when a man or a lady is ready for marriage. Also, graduation from an institution does not determine when you should marry. Below are some ways to know when you are prepared for marriage.

As a Man, how do I know I am ready for marriage?

1. When you are ready to be a spiritual head and a leader.

As a man, you must understand and accept full responsibility of becoming the spiritual head of your home. According to God's organogram, every man is supposed to be the spiritual head of the family. The wife and children should look up to the man for spiritual coverage and guidance. As a man, you are supposed to be the initiator of Bible study, prayer meetings and spiritual exercises in the family. As the spiritual head of the family, it is your duty to teach your family kingdom principles. It is your responsibility as the priest of the home to pray and command certain things to happen, especially when things are not working well in your home. As the spiritual head, it is your responsibility to set a spiritual template for your children. When negative things are happening to your family, it is your responsibility as the spiritual head to challenge those occurrences and speak over your family. A leader is someone who directs and leads a group of people to achieve a goal. As a man, you are the spiritual head and a leader of your home. Being a leader doesn't mean you should always think that you are right in everything. To function very as a leader, you must ask God for divine wisdom to lead and also, and it is also crucial to seek counsel from your beloved wife or partner. You must understand that leadership is not about being bossy but the ability to lead by example. In leading, you must bc humble. As a man, if you are not ready to be a spiritual head and a leader of your home, you are not prepared for marriage.

2. When you are ready to be a provider and a protector.

As a man, you must accept the responsibility of becoming a provider and a protector. ***(1 Timothy 5:8 NIV) "Anyone who does not provide for their relatives, and especially for their own household, has denied the faith and is worse than an unbeliever."*** The Bible clearly states that any man who cannot provide for his household is worse than an unbeliever. You don't have to get married before providing because you must become a provider before marriage. It is your responsibility to be a provider and a protector in the family. Respectfully speaking, any man who cannot provide for and protect his family is a failure. Your duty as a man is not limited to reproduction alone but to protect and provide. The ability to provide and protect is what makes you a father.

What are the things you provide as a man? You should be able to provide security for your wife and children. You should be able to provide financial and basic needs of the family. You should also be able to provide mentorship and guidance. You should be able to protect your family physically, emotionally, spiritually and socially. You should be able to cater for the family in all spheres of life. You should be able to provide accommodation, food and security for your family. Any man that cannot protect his family from physical, spiritual and mental forces is not ready for marriage. It is not until you are married that you become a provider and a protector; it starts even from your love relationship. Any man who is not ready to be a provider and a protector is not ready for marriage.

3. When you are ready to be a husband.

The role of a husband has been misunderstood in our world today. Many people think that the role of a husband is only about the sexual aspect; as crucial as it is, that is not all there is to be a husband. As a man, you must understand that you have a responsibility exclusively to your wife. It is your responsibility to provide for her emotional and psychological needs. You are a husband not necessarily when you get married, but when you are ready to perform the duty of a husband to your wife.

Many men think that their role as husbands is only in the pre-children era; that is wrong. You are not a husband only before the children come, but you are also a husband in post children's era. Many men are the spiritual head of their homes, providers, and protectors, but they are not good husbands to their wives. You must give your wife attention, love, emotional support, and satisfaction as a husband. You should be able to give your wife emotional security. So many men have deprived their wives of the love and attention that they need. Respectfully speaking, so many men out there, including men of God, politicians, businessmen, captains of industries, etc., have failed as a husband. They don't carry their wives along. Men must wake up because many women have been depressed because their husbands have deprived them of the love and attention they need. So, when you are ready to be a husband, you are prepared for marriage.

4. **When you are ready to plan for marriage, not just a wedding.**

A wedding is a ceremony of getting married, while marriage is a long-term relationship between two partners. A wedding is for hours, while marriage is forever. As a man, you must have wedding plans; you must have long term marriage plans. Any man who does not have plans is not going anywhere. Don't plan for a wedding that is for hours and forget to plan for a marriage that is for a lifetime. As a man intending to marry, you should have financial plans, spiritual plans, career goals etc. As a man, when you are ready to become a spiritual head, a provider and a protector, a husband and a marriage planner, then you are ready for marriage.

As a woman, how do I know I am ready for marriage?

1. When you are ready to be an intercessor and a prayerful woman.

You must understand that you have the responsibility of standing in the gap for your family. You must shape yourself to become a prayerful woman. It is your responsibility to intercede for your children and your husband. There are times when your family will be weak; it is your duty to stand in the gap in prayer for them. When things are not moving well in your home, put on your garments as an intercessor and gatekeeper of your family and pray against negative occurrences.

As a lady, when you are preparing for marriage, you are preparing to become an intercessor. The moment you notice that the devil is trying to sow a seed of stubbornness and disobedience in your children's lives, it is not the time to start flogging the children. It is the time that you have to rise as a watcher and an intercessor to confront the gate of darkness. You are prepared for marriage when you are ready to be an intercessor and a prayerful woman.

2. When you are ready to become a homemaker.

Some women are wives but not a homemaker. A homemaker is a woman who sacrifices to build her home. A man cannot build a home alone, so it is the duty of the woman to join make and build the home. As a woman, it is your responsibility to inculcate peace and love in your home.

As a co-home builder, you must keep your kitchen, toilet, and living room or sitting room clean at all times. There are so many women respectfully speaking whose kitchen, bathroom and living room are unhealthy. Your kitchen, toilet and living room will determine whether you are a homemaker or not. It is also your responsibility to cook for the family. Sadly, so many women have left that responsibility to their husbands. It is a different thing entirely if your husband decides to help you out in the kitchen, but you should know as a woman that it is your responsibility. A homemaker will sacrifice for the growth of her home. You should be able to inconvenience yourself for the comfort of your home. As a lady, when you are ready to become a homemaker, you are prepared for marriage.

3. When you are ready to become a virtuous woman and a wife.

You must accept the responsibility of becoming a virtuous woman and a wife. According to Proverbs 31, a virtuous woman is a woman who manages and leads her home with integrity, wisdom and discipline. All her virtues are channeled towards making her husband's life better. You are a wife when you understand your role and execute your responsibilities. Planted in every man is a king, and you have to bring out the king in your husband. Some women are killing the king in their husbands, don’t do so.

As a wife, you ought to be physically attractive to your husband. Men are always attracted to what they see. Don't dress abnormally or put on dirty clothes. Always dress decent and look attractive to your husband. Being attractive to your husband has nothing to do with nudity and deduction, but you must look good and presentable. Some couples whose marriage is just two years old, but the woman looks 60 years old already. This is one of the reasons why some men cheat on their wives; they go out looking for ladies who dress well and are attractive.

Nevertheless, I am not supporting that men should cheat on their wives under any circumstances, but you must learn to dress well and be physically attractive to your husband. Many women have taken their husbands for granted. They don't serve him food; there are some families where the children serve the husband food; it is alright if the woman is not at home. Some women don't honour and respect their husband, and some doesn't even submit. You must make your husband feel like a man. You should dress in such a way that he will be proud of you. Anytime you shout at your husband and dishonour him, you are killing the king in him. You must honour and bring out the king in him. Your responsibility as a wife is exclusive to your husband. When you are ready to be a virtuous woman and a wife, you are prepared for marriage.

4. When you understand, and you are ready to become a help meet.

(Gen 2:18 KJV) "And the Lord God said, it is not good that the man should be alone; I will make him a help meet for him." The Purpose God made a woman for the man is to be a helpmeet to the man and also to support him. As a woman, it is your responsibility to help and support your husband to achieve the family goals. Assist and support him spiritually, physically, financially, mentally, socially and emotionally. Don't leave all the family responsibilities for him alone just because he is the head of the family. You must assist and support him in all areas for the growth and progress of the family. There are so many women who are not help meet to their partners. Instead of supporting and helping him, some women become a liability to the man. You must understand that you were created to be a helpmeet to your husband. You must learn to encourage your husband, motivate him and inspire him. You are prepared for marriage when you understand and are ready to become a help meet.

You are ready for marriage when you are ready to become an intercessor, a homemaker, a virtuous woman and a wife and help meet.

CHAPTER EIGHT

Causes of Late Marriage.

Delay in marriage seems to be on the high side. One of the prevalent issues among singles worldwide today is that of late marriage. Many are so desperate and hopeless that they sometimes try to lure married men and women. It has become a global phenomenon that gives parents, relatives, men of God, and marriage counselors deep concern. Some have concluded that they can no longer get the person of their dreams. God is interested in every aspect of our lives. It is not God's will that we suffer unnecessary delays. Although according to (Matthew 19:10-12) not everyone will marry. Below are some of the reasons or causes of delay in marriage:

1. Confusion about God's timing and the will of God.

Many people have been scared of missing out on the will of God in marriage. We must understand that marriage is a covenant and not something you go into and come out of whenever you feel tired. There has been a lot of confusion about God's timing. And many people have been confused as to whether there is one particular person destined for them in marriage. Many people in our world today have been delayed in marriage because they are confused on the subject of God's timing and the will of God. One of the ways to understand God's timing is through the Holy Spirit. (Act 1:7-8) the Holy Spirit is key to helping you make the right decisions at the right time. The Holy Spirit is a revealer; he reveals God's timing.

2. Spiritual Problems.

This is one of the major causes of delays in marriages. There are so many people who have wanted to marry for some years now but can't figure out what the problem is; it could be spiritual Problems. Spiritual issues could be why you are struggling to love your partner. Some are under spells and satanic manipulations. Some were destined to marry many years ago but are still singles due to spiritual hindrances.

Some are suffering from ancestral curses, and it has caused the delay in marriages. Some have been covenanted into spiritual alters that have led to late marriages. To come out of this problem, you must surrender your life to Christ, have the requisite knowledge and engage in prayer and fasting.

3. Attitude.

A person's character determines who they are. Your behaviour contributes to the building of your future. Respectfully speaking, there are so many people who have flawed characters, which is why they have not found their life partner. Bad attitudes like; being arrogant as a lady, being disrespectful and proud. While as a man, bad attitudes like; lack of self-control, not accepting corrections, being irresponsible, etc. So many people go into a relationship, and in the short run, the relationship ends due to bad attitudes. Let's work on ourselves, develop and build a solid character.

4. Unreasonable Marriage requirements.

Many traditions have turned their ladies into business commodities by setting their marriage rites above reasonable standards. Many men love their partners and want to marry them but are unable because they cannot even afford one-quarter of the marriage rite. Today, there are so many places where the marriage rites are too high and unaffordable to some people. Respectfully speaking, so many traditional leaders and elders give out their daughters as if they are selling them out. All of these contributes to late marriages and delay in getting married.

5. Unnecessary Preferences and Indecision

There are so many people who are over-selective and have high expectations. For instance, a lady can decide that she must marry a guy who has a duplex, the wealthiest guy in the world, he must be fair or dark in complexion, a very tall guy, etc. Some guys have unreasonable expectations like; she must be a fair lady, be eloquent, have a pointed nose, be short, have a figure 8 and a physique, etc. All these expectations are not necessary and are unreasonable. Many people are experiencing a delay in marriage because of all these high and unreasonable expectations. Being over-selective is one of the reasons for late marriage. The majority of us focus on the minor and ignore the major. Let us cut off those unreasonable expectations and focus on what matters.

6. Financial Constraints.

Finance is essential in marriage, especially in some continents, where an early establishment is difficult. Many young men intend to have a degree before finding something to do but are unable due to delays in some institutions. Another factor is the high rate of unemployment. There are so many graduates around the world who have been searching for some lucrative jobs for over a decade now but are unable.

The economic downturn is putting stress on marriages at every income level. Financial problems can cause mayhem and bring many couples to the brink of divorce. Financial constraints are one of the major causes of late marriages and delays in getting married. To avoid late marriage due to financial conditions, ensure you don't depend solely on your certificate and learn a paying skill. Where possible, multiple income streams won't be a bad idea.

CHAPTER NINE

Biblical Principles of Choosing a Life Partner.

Marriage is the second greatest and most important decision you will make in your life, second only to the decision of knowing Christ. There have been a lot of tensions and confusion surrounding the concept of finding a life partner; there are pathways and principles in the scriptures to guide us. Some of us have been taught that the only way to choose a life partner is through visions, revelations and the prophetic. But most times, God won't come down face to face to tell you that this is the right person to marry. He provided us with a manual that is God's word to guide us.

MYTH OF CHOOSING A LIFE PARTNER.

A myth is a common misconception or a false belief. It is a concept held to be the truth but has no basis for its veracity. Below is the myth of choosing a life partner.

"God chooses the person he wants me to marry and has only one person for me". So many people have believed that God has one particular person for them. So many have even been taught in church that God has a specific person for us. We have been taught that we have to fast and pray until that person crosses our paths; this is a myth. Let's be very honest with ourselves because there are over six billion people globally. If there is this specific person that is right for you, what is the possibility of both of you crossing paths? There are thousands of people who are potential mates for you.

Many have also been taught that it's God who chooses their life partner. This is one of the causes of delay in marriages today. They believe that God will show or reveal their spouse to them in a vision, dreams, prophecy and other supernatural means. Some even believe that when they close their Bible and open it, any name that appears is their partner; this is a myth. If God is the one who chooses our life partner, then we are making him responsible for the failures of marriages and relationships. You must understand that God is not a liar, and he is not the cause of your broken heart and relationship. God doesn't break a heart; he mends a heart. Study your Bible, and you will find out that God doesn't choose mates for his people; it is man's responsibility to choose. (Genesis 2:18,21-24) God did not choose the woman for the man, and neither did he give the woman to him. God brought her to the man, and he accepted the woman without any compulsion. God doesn't choose our mates; the choice is ours.

The followings are the guides to choosing your life partner.

The Spiritual Aspect.

This is an essential aspect that two people should focus on to come together in one spirit. The will of God is that we marry who is genuinely born again. A believer and an unbeliever cannot work together. Spiritual intimacy occurs when two believers come together to share God's dealings with them. The spiritual aspect is the stage where spiritual intimacy is built. Someone who does not have a relationship with God cannot be your life partner as long as kingdom marriage is concerned. In this aspect, both partners must be spiritually mature to handle life issues. In this stage, both of you should be able to overcome sexual temptations and maintain purity. Anyone who cannot control his or herself sexually before marriage, might not be able to control his or her sexual desire even when he is married. The spiritual aspect is one of the important factors you must look out for when choosing a life partner. In this aspect, partners should learn where each other stands in terms of faith, worship and commitment to holy and righteous living as believers. If partners cannot agree on the spiritual aspect, there will be a problem.

The Soulical Aspect.

This aspect deals with intellect, will and emotions. This is where partners will begin to learn and understand each other's interests, purpose in life, personal goals, career goals, etc. This is the stage where they discuss their plans. They share their likes and dislikes in this aspect. A potential couple sits to discuss their personal goals, life purposes etc. For instance, if the man has the calling of

God upon his life, this is the stage where both of them will sit and discuss it. It is also the stage where the potential couple discusses their families, both the family they grew up with and the ones they intend to build. If there is mutual agreement at this stage, then there won't be a problem.

The Body or the Physical Aspect.

This aspect talks about the physical dimensions. The appearance of the person, even though this aspect is inferior compared to the two aspects above, it is still important to consider. This is the stage where you consider whether he is 'handsome' or she is 'beautiful'. In this stage, you consider the physical attractiveness, the heights, the complexion, the body physique etc. But you must understand that the physical aspect alone cannot sustain your marriage. The progression of Spirit, Soul and body is the pathway to a fruitful and successful marriage.

The Spirit, Soul and Body Combination;

When both partners agree on the spiritual ground and the Soulical level, the marriage can work. When the partners agree on the spiritual aspect and the physical level, the marriage can also work. When they don't agree spiritually and agree on both the soulical and physical level, the possibility of the marriage to work is very low.

Two indices are used to discern the right life partner;

1. Compatibility.

When the potential couples are not compatible, there is a high possibility of the marriage being in disaster. There must be similarities in ideologies. The couple must be compatible spiritually, physically, mentally, psychologically etc.; when there is no compatibility, the marriage won't work. There must be compatibility in parenting. Never marry someone you are not compatible with; otherwise, your marriage will be in jeopardy.

2. God's leading.

(Isaiah 30:21 KJV) "And thine ears shall hear a word behind thee, saying, this is the way, walk ye in it, when ye turn to the right hand, and when ye turn to the left." In choosing a life partner, you must trust God for his leading. You should be able to discern if it is God who is leading you or your emotions are leading you. Always expect and submit to the leadership of the Holy Spirit in choosing a life partner. When God lead you, there won't be any regrets. God cannot lead you into confusion. Submit to the Leadership of God, and he will direct your path.

CHAPTER TEN

Engagement.

This is the preparation time for marriage. Our society has neglected this stage. As followers of Christ, our standard is the word of God. Many believers don't understand the biblical view of engagement. Engagement is the first stage of marriage. The engagement period is a time for both the man and the woman to make practical preparations for joining themselves in marriage. It is also a period where the couple's families will come together to establish the marriage covenant.

In our world today, society has taken engagement for granted. Many people have illicit relationships with the opposite sex even when they are only engaged. From a kingdom perspective, when you are engaged, it is not right for you to involve in a romantic or sexual relationship with anyone because you are committed to another. Even though you are not fully married, your engagement has taken you from the realm of singleness to the realm of marriage. The moment you are engaged, you ought to be faithful to your fiancée because the union has already begun.

A clear example of the relationship between engagement and marriage is seen in the circumstance that surrounds the birth of Jesus. (Matthew 1:16-25) Mary was described in Verse 18 as ***"pledged to be married to Joseph".*** That is, she was engaged to Joseph. The engagement was taken seriously in Mary and Joseph's day. It should be taken seriously in our world because (Hebrews 13:8 KJV) says, ***"Jesus Christ is the same yesterday and today and forever."*** This implies that God never changes. The fact that engagement should be taken seriously doesn't mean that it is right for people who are engaged to have an affair with one another. The physical consummation of the marriage is reserved for after the wedding when the fullness of marriage begins.

Things to Plan for During Engagement (courtship) Period.

To many, engagement means going out for movies, ice cream, kissing, holding hands etc. Even though engaged couples do some of those things, it is not the primary aim of engagement. Some of those things are done in dating and courtship. Below are the things to plan for during the engagement period.

1. Building a Spiritual Foundation.

Couples are expected to lay a solid spiritual foundation for their marriage during the engagement period. Building a firm spiritual foundation is the most crucial aspect of building a solid marriage. The couple must plan to build a spiritual foundation. The engagement Period is also a season when couples discuss and plan the church they will attend. A couple must plan and ensure spiritual harmony in their marriage. The engagement period is when the couple has to come together to have a similar spiritual ideology.

2. Building Financial Stability.

This is one of the major problems in marriages today. Financial constraints have led to a lot of divorce in our world today. Any couple planning for marriage without a proper finance plan is headed for a disaster. Engagement is when the potential couple has to discuss their financial goals and strategies. What kind of business do you intend to embark on? What type of job will fit you both, and what are the ways you can build multiple streams of income? All these are to be discussed during the engagement.

3. Principles of Parenting.

This is another critical area couples need to plan for during the engagement period. It is also a time when couples discuss whether they want children, the number of children and biblical ways of proper upbringing. The potential couple should have a similar opinion on discipline. The potential couple must agree as to the disciplinary approach they intend to adopt on their children. The engagement period is a time when the potential couple should plan and understand the principle of parenting.

CONCLUSIONS

In Conclusion, there is no success without thorough preparations. Lack of preparation will always result in failure. You must trust God to build capacity. You must study and obey the word of God above all things in your life. You must also remain consistent in prayer during your season of preparation.

ABOUT THE BOOK.

Preparing for marriage is a book that will help you build capacity. It will make you understand the basic requirements for marriage. It contains some undiluted truth that will help sustain your relationship and marriage. This book teaches you to develop some excellent qualities that you should possess as a man or a woman preparing for marriage. In this book, you will discover that marriage is not a game of luck and chance but a product of careful planning, determination, focus and thorough preparation that will lead you to an extraordinary and fulfilled life on Earth. The book is a practical road map to achieving successful and glorious marriage. The book will help you understand when you are ready for marriage and the Biblical principles of choosing a life partner.

ABOUT THE AUTHOR

Ezekiel Ugbeda is a Gospel Preacher, a relationship and marriage counsellor. He is a motivational speaker. He has Bachelor's degree in Accounting in view in Ahmadu Bello University Zaria.

He is called with a mandate of bringing men to seek and follow Jesus Christ. He is a passionate lover of God. His goal is to see Jesus revealed and Jesus glorified.

www.ingramcontent.com/pod-product-compliance
Lightning Source LLC
LaVergne TN
LVHW050331160826
845677LV00014B/3590

9789787916704